To Lou.
–S.L.

North American edition © 2007 Bayard Canada Books Inc.

Originally published in France under the title *Mon encyclo des animaux*
Copyright © 2004 Éditions Milan – 300, rue Léon Joulin
31101 Toulouse Cedex 9 – France
www.editionsmilan.com
Printed in France

Publisher: Jennifer Canham
Editorial Director: Mary Beth Leatherdale
Editor: Katherine Dearlove
Production Manager: Lesley Zimic
Production Editor: Larissa Byj
Production Assistant: Kathy Ko

Thanks to David Field, Angela Keenlyside, Paul Markowski, Susan Sinclair, and Deb Yea.

We gratefully acknowledge the financial support of the Government of Canada through the
Book Publishing Industry Development Program (BPIDP) for our publishing activities.

 Conseil des Arts   Canada Council
du Canada   for the Arts

Library and Archives Canada Cataloguing in Publication

Ledu, Stéphanie
    ChickaDEE animal adventures : discover the world's amazing
animals / written by Stéphanie Ledu ; translated by Mark Stout.

Includes index. Translation of: Mon encyclo des animaux.
ISBN-13 978-2-89579-173-7
ISBN-10 2-89579-173-2

    1. Animals--Encyclopedias, Juvenile. I. Stout, Mark II. Title.

QL49.L4313 2007   j590.3   C2007-902925-6

Made in Spain
Produced by Éditions Milan - Toulouse - France

Owlkids Publishing
10 Lower Spadina Ave., Suite 400
Toronto, Ontario M5V 2Z2
Ph: 416-340-2700
Fax: 416-340-9769

Publisher of

chirp   chickaDEE   OWL
www.owlkids.com

chickaDEE Animal Adventures

Stéphanie Ledu

Translation: Mark Stout

Owl kids

Table of Contents

In the
Country

Farm animals like cows and
chickens share the countryside
with many different wild animals.
Birds, bugs, and other little
creatures all find homes and food
in farmland's fields and trees.

Farm Animals

**Every animal has its own part to play
in the busy world of the farm.**

The Goat

Goats love to play
and climb on rocks.
They also love to eat,
munching on tender
leaves, tree bark,
and even flowers.
Farmers milk the
nanny (female) goats
and use the milk
to make cheese.

Billy (male) goats have long beards growing from their chins. Nanny (female) goats have little goatees. Both male and female goats can have horns.

The Donkey

Donkeys can carry people or heavy loads on their backs. The gentle animals are often called stubborn because they won't do anything they think is dangerous.

Donkeys have excellent hearing and
can turn their big ears in every direction.

The Sheep

During the winter, sheep grow a thick coat of wool to keep warm. In the summer, the wool is cut off to be washed, spun, dyed, and made into yarn for sweaters and hats.

If one sheep runs away, the others will follow.

The Pig

Pigs have a huge appetite. They'll eat almost anything, including fruit, seeds, and vegetable peelings. Their meat is used to make ham, sausage, and more.

A pig is one of the most intelligent animals on a farm.

The Cow

When a dairy cow gives birth to a calf, her udder produces milk. The farmer milks her to keep the milk coming after the calf is grown. People drink cow's milk and use it to make butter, yogurt, and cheese.

Cows graze on grass, hay, shrubs, and grains.

Farmyard Birds

All sorts of birds strut around the farmyard. Most of them make their homes in pens, buildings that look like large sheds.

The Goose

The male goose is called a gander. The fuzzy babies are called goslings. Geese wander around the farmyard, eating fresh grass. Their light, warm feathers are used to fill duvets and pillows.

The goose keeps watch over the farmyard and honks loudly if she spots an enemy.

The Guinea Fowl

Guinea fowl are bad-tempered, noisy birds. They chase chickens around the farmyard and may try to bite them!

Farmers like guinea fowl because they eat pesky garden insects without hurting the plants.

Tom (male) turkeys strut and fan their tail feathers, showing off to the turkey hens (females).

The Duck

Ducks swim around the farm's pond searching the water for plants and insects to eat. Ducks are good swimmers but waddle slowly on land.

From birth, fluffy little ducklings follow their mother everywhere.

The Turkey

A turkey has no feathers on its head. On its neck hangs a caruncle, a red pouch that swells up when the turkey makes a gobbling noise. Turkeys eat just about anything, including grasses, berries, grains, and bugs.

The Emu

Emus are big birds that stand taller than an average person. They can't fly, but they can run as fast as cars driving on neighbourhood streets.

After the female emu lays her eggs, the male sits on them and cares for the chicks after they hatch.

The Rooster and the Hen

Cluck, cluck, cluck! Cock-a-doodle-doo! Hens and roosters make lots of noise as they peck their food in the farmyard.

The rooster watches over the farmyard, ready to defend the hens. Every morning, he crows at the top of his voice to let other roosters know he's the toughest bird in the yard.

In the Egg

Almost every day, the hen lays an egg in the henhouse straw. If she's mated with a rooster, she sits on the eggs to keep them warm. Then, one day, cute little chicks hatch out of their shells.

As soon as they hatch, chicks scurry about looking for food.

The rooster has a large red crest on his head and a wattle beneath his beak. The hen has a smaller crest and wattle.

Garden Visitors

**Little animals often visit the garden to sneak
a bite of the fruit and vegetables growing there.**

The Snail

On rainy days, snails like
to come out for a snack
of lettuce or other leaves.
When the sun comes out,
they head back to the
shelter of their shells to
keep from drying out. In
the winter, they sleep in the
ground or under a rock.

The two little black specks on the
end of a snail's long tentacles are its eyes.

The Rabbit

Rabbits have powerful back legs
built for jumping. They nibble
constantly on leaves, grass, bulbs,
and tree bark to wear down their
teeth, which never stop growing.

Rabbits can hear very quiet sounds
with their big ears.

The Skunk

Skunks defend themselves from enemies by blasting them with a stinky spray. The spray can travel two or three metres (yards). Skunks are good at hitting their targets.

Skunks sleep all day in underground burrows, coming out at dusk to look for a meal of insects, fish, fruit, leaves, or nuts.

Backyard Birds

Lots of birds fly around the countryside. They're easy to watch, and they do lots of interesting things.

The Chickadee

The chickadee hops from branch to branch looking for insect eggs, insects, and spiders to eat. Chickadees help keep the number of bugs in forests and orchards from getting too big.

The plump black-capped chickadee is easy to spot with its black cap and black bib under its beak.

The Red-Winged Blackbird

Red-winged blackbirds fly south for the winter, often travelling in flocks of a thousand birds.

Red-winged blackbirds make a meal of seeds, grains, nuts, worms, or bugs. They can even catch insects that fly by.

The robin gets up early in the morning to sing. It also sings in the evening.

The Robin

The robin sings loudly, warning other birds to stay away from its home! When a robin wants to frighten its enemies, it puffs up its red feathers.

The Magpie

This bird is called the "thieving magpie" because it likes to grab shiny objects like bottle caps or tin foil and fly away with them to decorate its nest.

In the garden, magpies eat worms and fruit, but they also eat bugs from the backs of larger animals.

In the Farm Fields

Many animals build their homes in the fields of tall summertime crops. Others animals like to hunt there.

The Northern Harrier

Harriers, which are a type of hawk, seem to glide through the air. They fly low, looking for mice and other rodents. When they spot one, they dive straight at it, talons open wide.

To hide her young, the harrier hen makes her nest in the middle of a field.

The Weasel

Weasels live wherever they can find mice, birds, rabbits, insects, and berries to eat. Small and flexible, a weasel can slip through a hole the size of a nickel!

The weasel can smell a fox, its enemy, from far away.

The harvest mouse runs upside down along plant stems. It can even hang by its tail, just like an acrobat!

The Harvest Mouse

The tiny harvest mouse lives in Europe and Asia. It builds a ball-shaped nest small enough to fit in the palm of a human hand. Farmers don't like the mice because they munch on crops like corn and wheat.

In the Meadow

**Sheep and cattle roam the meadow, grazing on plants.
But many other creatures also make their homes in the meadow.**

The Bee

When a bee finds a meadow full of flowers, it does a special dance to tell other bees how to get there. Bees sometimes fly far from their hive to gather nectar and pollen from the flowers. Pollen is a yellow powder, and nectar is a sweet liquid. Bees use nectar to make honey.

Bees carry pollen on their hind legs in special pouches called pollen baskets.

The Earthworm

Earthworms swallow dirt as they tunnel through the earth. Some go up to the surface to get rid of poop through the tip of their tail, leaving a bunch of poopy little coils all over the meadow.

Earthworms have no eyes. It's hard to tell their tail from their head, which is just a bit pointier.

The Ladybug

The ladybug's red colour warns birds and spiders that it tastes terrible. Gardeners like ladybugs because they gobble up aphids, little green insects that are harmful to plants.

Ladybugs have little hooks on the ends of their legs to help them crawl over plants to find food.

The Garter Snake

Garter snakes often live near water where they can find frogs and fish to eat. They hibernate all winter, curled up with other garter snakes in animal burrows, under rock piles, or in tree stumps.

Garter snakes come in many different colours. They can be black, brown, grey, or green and have yellow, blue, brown, or green stripes.

The Grasshopper

Grasshoppers have spring-like hind legs to help them jump high. They hop into bushes and long grasses to find leaves to eat.

Green grasshoppers are hard to see when they're hiding in the leaves and grass.

By the Hedge

A hedge is a great hiding place for animals. It's like a fence made of plants and trees between farm fields.

The Dormouse

The dormouse, which lives in Europe, has a hearty appetite. It eats the tasty blackberries and hazelnuts it finds in the hedges. To get to its food, the dormouse runs along very slender branches — even thorny ones!

It's hard to surprise a dormouse. As soon as it hears a noise, it scurries into hiding.

The Red-Legged Partridge

The red-legged partridge pecks at seeds and bugs inside the hedge. The female lays eggs in the bushes to hide them, but sometimes a fox finds and eats them.

The partridge is a wild hen with a red beak and red feet.

The small tortoiseshell butterfly often lays its eggs underneath a nettle leaf.

The Small Tortoiseshell Butterfly

Like many butterflies, the small tortoiseshell butterfly finds shelter in the hedge when it rains. As soon as the sun comes out, the butterfly unfolds its wings to warm them before flying away.

In the City

Animals make their homes throughout the city, both indoors and out. Houses, parks, and yards all bustle with animal life.

Hidden in the City

Animals find food, shelter, and warmth in houses. They settle on the roof, in out-of-the-way corners, and in the yard.

Mice go inside houses looking for warm places to build their nests.

The Mouse

Mice are tiny and flexible. They twist and squeeze their way through a house, making a mess as they gnaw on paper, fabric, and even soap. They leave their poop everywhere.

A rat weighs about as much as ten mice!

The Rat

Rats are excellent swimmers and often live in the sewer. Because they spread germs and chew on everything, people try to get rid of them. But it isn't easy. In a year, a female rat can give birth to as many as sixty babies!

If a wall lizard gets caught by the tail, it can drop its tail and run away. Then it can grow a new tail.

The Wall Lizard

Wall lizards cling to city and country walls, basking in the warm sun. At the slightest danger, they disappear into any little hole they can find. But the bold creatures quickly come out again.

The Pipistrelle

Pipistrelle bats are tiny. Their bodies are as small as an adult's thumb! During the day, they sleep upside down in a barn or attic. At night, they fly in groups to hunt insects.

When night falls, pipistrelle bats zigzag their way through the sky.

Birds in the Park

Many birds spend their days in the park where there are ponds and rivers for swimming and fishing, and plenty of trees for shelter.

The Swan

Swans seem to glide on the water using their flipper-like feet to paddle forward. The big, heavy birds have to beat their wings and run along the water's surface before they can take flight.

Baby swans take naps or ride on the backs of full-grown swans.

The Mallard Duck

Quack, quack! Ducks are talkative birds. As soon as they hatch, the brown and yellow ducklings follow their mother in single file. If one gets out of line, she scolds and goes after it.

The male duck has an emerald-green head and neck. The female is brown.

Peafowl

To attract a peahen (female), the peacock (male) spreads its tail feathers out in a huge fan. This is called fanning. The round spots on his feathers look like big eyes.

Only the peacock (male) is colourful. The peahen (female) has brown feathers.

The Sparrow

Sparrows live anywhere people do, in cities and in towns. They perch in trees together to sleep, and they land on the ground to find seeds, fruit, and insects to eat.

This sparrow is a female. The male has rings around its eyes and a black bib on its throat.

Huge flocks of pigeons live in cities all over the world. In many places, it's against the law to feed them.

The Pigeon

In the wilderness, pigeons live perched on cliffs. They also feel at home on tall city buildings, although their poop is harmful to the stonework of buildings and statues.

The Cat

In the house, a cat walks around on velvety paws.
But the animal is a hunter with a wild side, too.
A cat's sharp claws come out in the yard.

Super Kitty

Cats can smell odours from far away and have excellent hearing and eyesight, even at night. With its flexible body, a cat can go almost everywhere. And with its sharp teeth and claws, cats are a frightening enemy for birds, mice, and lizards.

Cats try to catch flies and butterflies.
They hunt and play at the same time.

Cats walk along fences, the tops of walls, and roofs. They have a good sense of balance.

Some cats live their lives indoors. The curious creatures like to sit near windows to see what's going on outside.

Pets at Home

Many animals live with people, in houses or apartments. Which one is your favourite?

The Dog

Dogs are intelligent companions and can tell whether you're happy or sad. They are energetic and need to go for a walk every day. In cities, dogs should be kept on a leash.

Dogs love to have fun chasing a ball, tugging a stick, or rolling around in the grass.

The Hamster

Hamsters are active creatures, especially at night, and they make lots of noise running on a wheel in their cage. They have sharp front teeth, which never stop growing.

Hamsters store food in the pouches of their cheeks.

A bowl is too small for a goldfish! It needs an aquarium.

The Goldfish

Goldfish make good pets, but they also swim around ponds in parks where they grow to be quite large. During the winter, these hardy fish can stay alive, even beneath a layer of ice.

The Zebra Finch

The pretty little zebra finch comes from Australia. It sings all day long and likes to play on its swing or bathe.

The male zebra finch is easy to spot. It has a bright red beak and a striped breast.

Household bugs

These little monsters don't wait for an invitation. They creep right into the kitchen, bathroom, or attic. They might look scary, but these bugs are more afraid of you.

The Ant

Ants often make their home in a woodpile or in the wall of a house. They walk in single file through the kitchen looking for something sweet.

Ants are small but strong. Some ants are able to carry objects fifty times their body weight.

The Spider

A spider makes its web silk in a special pouch under its belly. It spins a web on the ceiling then waits for flying insects to fall into its trap.

This hairy little spider is called a house spider. It lives both inside houses and out in nature.

The Wasp

Hundreds of wasps live together in a group called a colony. They build nests made from chewed-up wood and saliva in places like a hollow log or on the side of a house. The sturdy nests are as light as paper.

Even if you're frightened, don't wave your arms at a wasp. Wasps sting to defend themselves.

The Housefly

Bzzzz.... Houseflies make a lot of noise! They rub their front legs together to clean up. And they have huge eyes to look out for spiders and birds, which like to eat flies.

The housefly unrolls its long tongue to suck up food.

Fresh Water

Fish, birds, and many other
animals make their homes in the water
and on the banks of freshwater
rivers and streams.

Small Rivers

Many creatures live in flowing rivers and along riverbanks. You might see some of them if you go on a nature hike.

The Fire Salamander

Spotted salamanders live near forest streams. They hide under rocks all day and only come out to hunt for worms and bugs when it's dark.

The salamander's bright colours warn enemies that its skin is poisonous.

The Trout

Trout live in the running waters of cold, clear rivers. Each fish guards its own area and has favourite spots for hunting or resting.

Trout will feast on almost anything, from black flies and worms to salamanders and smaller fish.

The Dragonfly

Dragonflies can see in almost every direction with their big eyes. The speedy insects dart around, gobbling up flies, mosquitoes, and butterflies as they go.

From tip to tip, dragonfly wings are wider than a kid's hand.

The Raccoon

At night, raccoons splash around the riverbank, using their front paws to search for worms or small fish hiding under stones. The masked animals grab their prey with flexible fingers and pop them into their mouth.

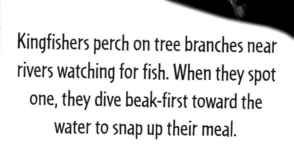

The Kingfisher

The kingfisher uses its long, pointy beak to dig a tunnel-shaped nest along the riverbank, which it lines with brittle fish bones and scales.

Kingfishers perch on tree branches near rivers watching for fish. When they spot one, they dive beak-first toward the water to snap up their meal.

Raccoons like to live close to the water. During the day, these excellent climbers sleep in trees and hollow logs.

Marshes and Ponds

Water collects in low spots on the land. Plants grow and animals move in. A whole little world comes to life.

The Heron

Standing tall in the water, a heron can stay still for a long time. Suddenly, it whips its head forward to catch a fish or a frog with its scissor-sharp beak.

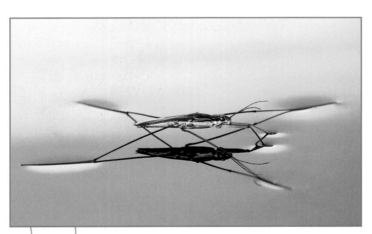

The feather-light water strider slides over the water surface like a skater.

The Water Strider

Also called a "pond skater," the water strider has six legs — two short ones and four very long ones. Tiny, waterproof hairs form air cushions on the ends of its legs to keep the insect afloat.

The grey heron can be nearly one metre (yard) tall, almost as tall as a six-year-old kid.

Map turtles pile onto logs or large rocks to bask in the sun.

The Map Turtle

Map turtles are named for the markings on their shells that look like the lakes and rivers on a map. In the winter, map turtles burrow into the mud to hibernate.

The Mosquito

Only female mosquitoes bite animals and people for their blood. The blood feeds the mosquito's eggs, which she lays on the water's surface. Male mosquitoes slurp up nectar from flowers.

The female mosquito's stinger is as sharp as a needle.

The Tree Frog

Tree frogs live near marshes in trees and tall grasses.
But like most frogs, they hatch and grow up in the water.

The Great Change

Tree frogs lay their eggs in the water. Tiny tadpoles hatch and gradually grow four legs. When they lose their tail, the tadpoles have become tree frogs.

This tadpole is already quite grown up. Its hind legs have grown out.

Ribbit, ribbit! On spring evenings, the tree frog puffs up his throat and croaks loudly to attract females.

To get around, tree frogs hop from one plant stem to another. Large, sticky discs on their toes keep them from falling.

Rivers in Europe

Large rivers flow more slowly than small ones, and their water is not as clear. At the end of their journey, they flow into the sea. Meet the animals that live in large European rivers.

The Beaver

European beavers dig burrows on the banks of large rivers. A beaver family's burrow can have as many as fifteen doors hidden below the water's surface.

A beaver's flat tail and webbed feet help it swim. Beavers slap their tails on the water to warn others of danger.

The Otter

Otters are playful and love to chase fish. They come out at nightfall and roam over a large area, marking the boundaries of their territory with their poop, which stinks like fish!

Otters have a flat head, small ears, long whiskers, and webbed paws.

Flamingos get their colour from all the pink shrimp they eat.

The Flamingo

In France, flamingos flock together in large groups called pats where the Rhône river flows into the Mediterranean Sea. They suck water through their beaks, where a row of spines traps their food.

The Pike

The pike is a large fish with powerful jaws and seven hundred razor-sharp teeth. The hearty eater feasts on insects, other fish, frogs, and even small ducks.

Pike can gobble up fish that are half their size. But it takes them several days to digest their big meal.

Rivers in Africa

Elephants, lions, zebras, and other animals all visit the river to drink and bathe. Some animals live there all the time.

The Nile Crocodile

A Nile crocodile sometimes looks like a floating log. But this dangerous animal is always on the lookout for a meal of birds or gazelles. The crocodile can spring from the water in an instant to catch its prey, which it drags underwater to drown.

The Nile crocodile is as long as a big car.

The Hippopotamus

Hippopotamuses graze at night and rest in the water during the day. From time to time, they dive down to stretch their legs with a walk along the riverbed. Underwater, their ears and nostrils clamp shut to keep the water from getting in.

Hippopotamuses sometimes leave the water to sunbathe.

The pelican can hold up to four kilograms (nine pounds) of fish in its pouch-like beak.

The Pelican

Pelicans swim side by side and beat their wings on the water to hunt for fish. They trap the fish and force them toward the riverbank, where the big birds scoop them up in their beaks.

On the PrairieS

Huge herds share wide-open grasslands with fearsome four-legged hunters. Hiding places are hard to find, so animals have to be strong, smart, or swift to survive.

The Great Plains

Animals large and small live on the Great Plains, the vast North American prairies that stretch from Alberta to Manitoba and south to Texas in the United States.

Cowbirds eat pesky insects from the bison's back.

The Bison

Bison gallop over the plains in search of fresh grass to graze on. In winter, they scrape the snow with their heads and hooves, looking for something to eat.

The Black-Footed Ferret

Black-footed ferrets are smaller than cats. They sneak into prairie dog burrows at night to eat any prairie dogs they can catch. Black-footed ferrets then raise their babies in the prairie dogs' empty dens.

Black-footed ferrets usually live underground, but sometimes they come out to warm themselves in the sun.

Prairie dogs recognize each other by sniffing and touching their teeth together.

The Prairie Dog

Prairie dogs live together in groups of as many as several thousand animals. They share underground tunnels and heaped entrance mounds called a prairie dog town. Guards stand on the mounds, ready to call out if danger is near.

The HorSe

Most horses live with people. But mustangs are wild animals that gallop freely over North America's Great Plains.

Mustangs run in herds, groups of horses made up of a stallion (male), several mares (females), and their foals (babies).

The Mustang

During the winter, the mustang's coat grows longer for extra warmth, like a winter blanket. When the wind blows hard, the herd huddles together to keep warm. They dig through the snow with their hooves, looking for grass to eat.

Sometimes a horse will nibble on a friend's neck. This is how horses show each other affection.

When a horse senses danger, it gallops away. Since it has no fangs or claws, running is the best way for the animal to protect itself. When it can't run, a horse will stand and fight.

The Pampas

In South America, the endless grassy plains are called the pampas. Millions of cattle are raised on this rainy, green land where there is lots of grass to eat. Other creatures live here, too.

The Maned Wolf

The maned wolf looks a little like a tall red fox. Its long legs give it height to spot prey in the pampas grasses. The wolf prefers to travel alone and keeps its distance from people.

The maned wolf is from the same family as dogs, foxes, coyotes, and other wolves.

The Armadillo

The armadillo's head, body, and tail are covered with a hard shell to protect it from enemies. Some armadillos can roll up into a ball to protect their faces and soft stomachs.

There are twenty different kinds of armadillos. This dwarf armadillo is about as long as this book.

The giant anteater has a long head and body. It's about the size of a German shepherd dog.

The Giant Anteater

Anteaters break open ant and termite hills with their long claws. Then they lap up insects with their sticky tongues, which can be longer than a kid's arm! The animals eat about 30,000 insects every day.

The Chinchilla

Chinchillas are excellent climbers. To escape from enemies, the animals run and jump easily over rocks to find a hiding place. If a wildcat or a bird of prey catches a chinchilla, a tuft of the chinchilla's fur can come loose in the enemy's claws, leaving the animal free to run away.

Chinchillas have big ears, a long tail, and beautiful, soft, grey fur.

Savannah Giants

**The grasslands of Africa are called the savannah.
Many large animals make their homes in the tall grasses
that become green during the rainy season.**

The Rhinoceros

The rhinoceros has poor eyesight. When a rhino feels nervous, it charges straight ahead to scare its enemies away or injure them with its big horn. A rhinoceros may be heavy, but it can run fast.

The white rhinoceros (above) spends its days grazing. In the evening, it drinks water and soaks in a mud bath.

The Ostrich

The male ostrich is the world's biggest bird, and the female lays the world's biggest eggs. Ostriches are too heavy to fly, but they run quickly on their strong legs.

Male ostriches are black and white. Females are grey.

The elephant is the biggest animal that lives on dry land.

The Elephant

Elephants' tusks are teeth that never stop growing. The animals use their flexible trunks to breathe, put grass in their mouths, drink, and take showers. Elephant cows (females) and calves (babies) live together in herds. Bull (male) elephants often live alone.

The Giraffe

When a giraffe is born, it is already taller than a full-grown person. With its long neck and black tongue, a giraffe can reach tender leaves high in the treetops, beyond the reach of any other animal.

Giraffes are the tallest animals. A giraffe could look into the second-floor window of a house!

Savannah Hunters

In the savannah, danger is never far away. Big cats are fierce hunters with sharp claws and teeth.

The Leopard

Leopards hunt their favourite prey of monkeys, wildebeest, and gazelle at night. When they kill a big animal, such as a gazelle, they're strong enough to drag it into a tree to keep other hunters from stealing a bite.

Perched high in a tree, the leopard keeps watch for a while, then takes a little nap.

The Cheetah

Hidden in the grass, the cheetah creeps up on its prey without a sound then leaps into action! The cheetah is the fastest of all animals, running as fast as a car on a highway. But cheetahs can only run at their top speed for about ten seconds before they need to slow down.

The muscular cheetah is built for running on its long legs.

The Lion and the Lioness

A group of lions is called a pride. The females are the pride's hunters. But when they make a kill, the stronger males eat first.

The male lion has a mane, while the lioness has none.

Savannah Grazers

The African savannah has enough grass to feed huge herds of animals. Often, thousands of animals graze in the same area.

The Zebra

Zebras like to mix with gazelle herds. When they stick together, they stand a better chance of spotting and defending themselves against a lioness. When a zebra is attacked, it kicks its attacker with its powerful hooves.

Each zebra has its own individual set of stripes.

The Wildebeest

At the beginning of the dry season, wildebeest go on a long journey in search of water and tender grass. When they cross big rivers, they have to watch out for crocodiles waiting to eat them.

The wildebeest grazes on grass and will also eat tree leaves when grass is hard to find.

These springboks are on the lookout for their enemy, the cheetah.

The Springbok

Springboks are part of the antelope family. When an attacking cat is near, springboks jump up and down to frighten the attacker and warn other springboks. The jumping is called pronking. The strong animals can jump as high as a tall person.

The Cape Buffalo

The horns of a cape buffalo bull (male) look like a helmet on his forehead. If lions attack a cape buffalo from the bull's herd, he lowers his horns and charges straight at the attackers.

Buffalo calves have a woolly coat and big ears, just like the grown-ups.

In the FOrest

All kinds of animals use forests to build homes, hide from enemies, and find food to eat. These bustling woodlands are full of life.

At the Forest's Edge

When night falls, sounds of snapping twigs and rustling leaves fill the air. Many forest animals are just waking up.

The Red Fox

Foxes often make their homes in the dens of badgers or rabbits. They hunt in the evening, sniffing the ground to catch the scent of their prey. They also climb trees to steal eggs from birds' nests.

The red fox eats a variety of different things, including insects, berries, birds, and small animals.

The Badger

Badgers live together in large dens with many entrances. The dens are called setts. When threatened, badgers roll onto their backs and show their sharp claws.

In the evening, badgers go looking for a meal of fruit, roots, mushrooms, birds, frogs, or bugs.

Every year, the stag (male deer) loses its antlers.
The next year, the antlers grow back with more points.

The Deer

In the fall, the stag (male) bellows loudly to attract a doe (female). This is the rutting call. Stags battle antler to antler to show the doe which animal is the strongest.

The Wild Boar

Wild boars, which are a kind of wild pig, live in many parts of the world. The hungry animals root for worms with their snouts, leaving the forest floor dug up wherever they go.

The female boar is called a sow. Sows have litters of between four and eight babies.

In the Trees

Forest treetops are full of activity. Birds and insects lay their eggs in trees. Small animals find shelter in the trunks and branches.

The stag beetle is a large insect that buzzes loudly when it flies.

The Stag Beetle

When two stag beetles meet, they fight with their mouths. Each tries to grab the other and push it off the tree. The winner gets to mate with the female.

The Tawny Owl

At night, the tawny owl flies silently from its nest in a hollow tree to hunt for mice. It can hear their footsteps from far away. It also has large eyes and excellent eyesight.

Many male owls have plumes (large feathers) on top of their heads. Female owls do not.

The Squirrel

Squirrels bury many nuts to eat during the cold winter months. Sometimes, when they forget where they've hidden their nuts, the nuts sprout and grow into trees!

Squirrels use their tails to shade themselves from the sun during the day and to keep themselves warm at night.

The Wolf

Wolves make their homes in forests across North America and eastern Europe. But they also live on the prairies and the Far North's frozen tundra.

"Owoooo...." Wolves howl to let other wolves know where they are. The wolf pack howls back in response.

Leaders of the Pack

A group of wolves, called a pack, is led by a top male and a top female. They bare their teeth to show other wolves they're the leaders. The rest of the pack lower their heads, lay their ears flat against their heads, and keep their tails low to show obedience.

When wolves go off to hunt, the mother wolves stay behind to watch their pups. The hunters will bring them meat to eat.

Wolves hunt all night long. In the morning, they find a hiding place in the forest where they can sleep.

The Tropical Forest

In the warm, rainy forests of South America, trees and other plants grow to be huge. Different animals live on every level of the forest: on the ground, on tree branches, and in the treetops.

The Sloth

Sloths sleep almost all the time. They hold onto a branch with their big claws and snooze hanging upside down. When they wake up, they creep from branch to branch. The sloth is the slowest mammal on the planet.

Scarlet macaws pair up with one mate for life. The mates stick together and are rarely alone.

The Scarlet Macaw

Scarlet macaws are expert tree-climbers. They jab their sharp claws and pointy beaks into tree trunks to help them climb.

The sloth can be difficult to see. The animal sits as still as a statue and its fur is the colour of tree branches.

The Toco Toucan

The toco toucan's beak is large but light. The toucan uses it to grab fruit or other birds' eggs. It tosses the fruit or egg pieces into the air, then swallows them.

Noisy toco toucans fly through the jungle in small flocks of about six birds.

The Trap Door Spider

Trap door spiders don't spin webs to trap their prey. Instead, they live in a den hidden behind a trap door, jumping out to eat crickets, moths, beetles, and grasshoppers when they pass by.

Trap door spiders build emergency exits into their burrows so they can escape if an enemy invades.

The Emerald Tree Boa

During the day, emerald tree boas wrap themselves around tree branches to sleep. At night, they hang from the branch, ready to whip out and catch birds that wander too close.

Emerald tree boas are red at birth. They turn green as they grow into adulthood.

The Asian Jungle

These animals all live deep in the jungles of Asia. They look for safe places to live, far away from people.

The Tiger

Tigers' stripes help the big cats hide in the high grass. And with soft pads on their paws, tigers can sneak up silently on their prey of deer, buffalo, and wild boars. Because of their razor-sharp teeth and claws, tigers are frightening hunters.

Tigers are the world's biggest cats. They live in the jungle or on the savannah.

The Giant Panda

Giant pandas live in the jungles of China where bamboo grows. They munch on bamboo leaves and shoots almost all day long. It takes a lot of leaves to fill a panda!

The panda is a great tree climber and even likes to do somersaults.

Orangutans are great apes with red fur. They live on the islands of Borneo and Sumatra in southern Asia.

The Orangutan

Orangutans are the biggest tree-dwelling mammals on Earth. They're as large as a ten-year-old kid. They look for fruit as they swing from tree to tree, grabbing hold of branches with their hands and feet.

The Forests of Africa

The forests of Africa are full of animals living in the trees and on the ground.

Gorillas, which are bigger than people, are too big to climb trees.

The Gorilla

Gorillas are the biggest, strongest apes. But they are gentle giants. Male gorillas sometimes beat their chests to scare off enemies and protect their families.

Mother chimpanzees are affectionate with their young. A young chimp depends on its mother for three or four years.

The Chimpanzee

Chimpanzees are clever. They can crack nuts with a rock or make an umbrella out of a broad leaf. Chimps sleep high in cozy treetop nests that they build every night.

Chameleons puff up to frighten enemies, and they can easily change colour to blend in with their surroundings and hide.

The Chameleon

Chameleons sit motionless on branches, catching insects with their long, slender, sticky tongues. A chameleon's tongue is the same length as the rest of its body!

The Ring-Tailed Lemur

Ring-tailed lemurs live only in Madagascar, an African island. They take giant leaps from branch to branch, with baby lemurs holding onto their mothers' fur so they won't fall.

Ring-tailed lemurs hold their long, striped tails high in the air.

The Forests of Australia

Most Australian animals are very different from animals anywhere else. They've always lived on this huge island, far from the world's other animals.

Lorikeets are noisy chatterboxes.

The Lorikeet

Lorikeets are part of the parrot family. They live in big forest flocks called companies, but they also come into gardens to eat fruit. Their tongues are bristly like toothbrushes for gathering nectar and pollen from plants.

Platypuses dive to the bottoms of rivers to dig in the mud for shrimp or earthworms with their soft bills.

The Platypus

What a funny animal! The platypus has fur, a bill like a duck, and webbed feet. The female platypus lays eggs. When the babies hatch, they lick the milk that flows over their mother's fur.

Koalas only come down from their trees to find another tree with more leaves.

The Koala

Koalas move around quickly by making short hops or slowly by walking on all fours. They spend their days munching on eucalyptus leaves. The fragrant leaves are poisonous to people but they don't hurt koalas.

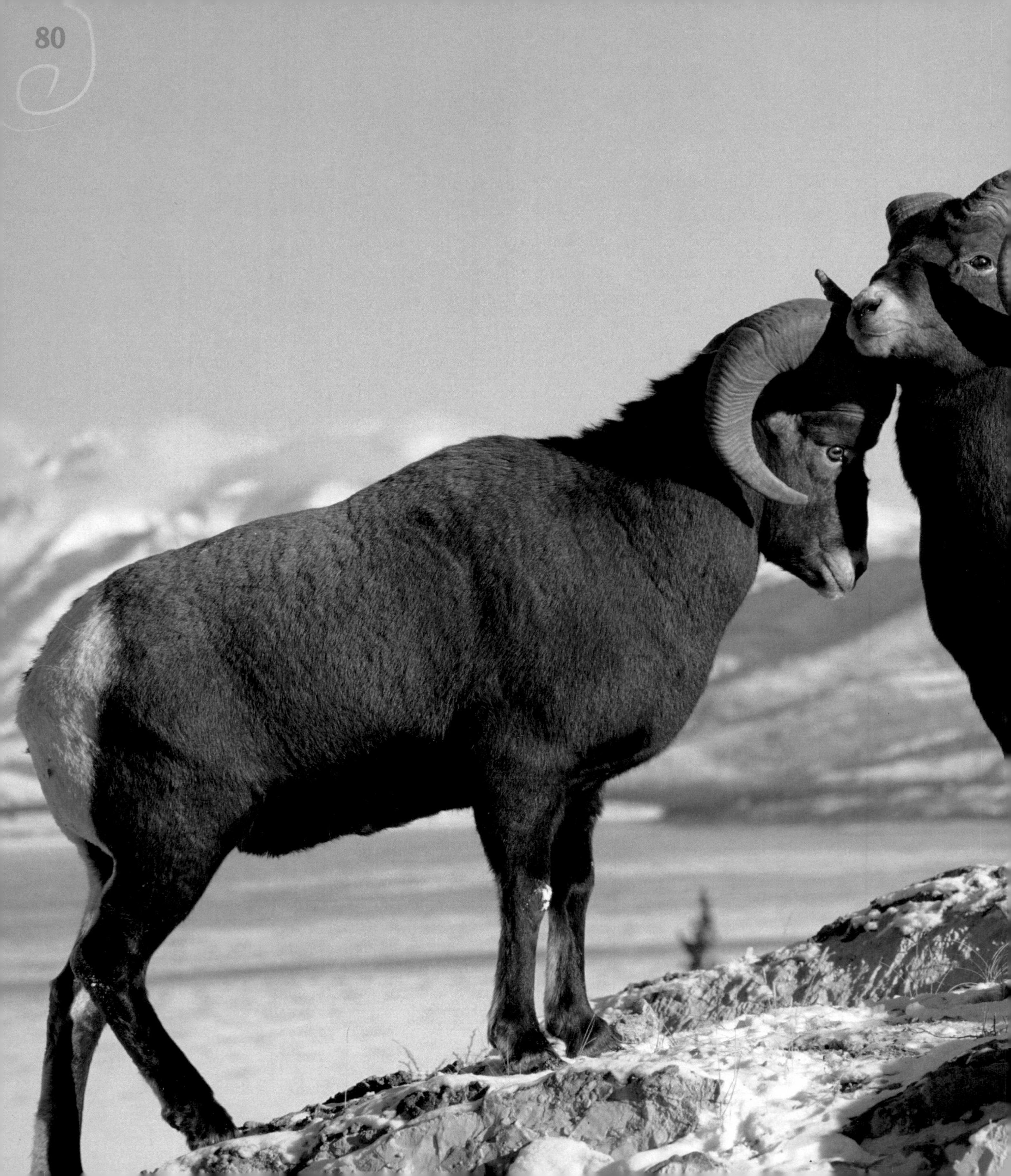

In the MOUNTAINS

Sure-footed animals brave the rugged landscapes of mountains all over the world. Finding food and shelter can be tough during frosty mountain winters.

The Himalayas

The Himalayas are the world's highest mountains. Very few plants can grow on the mountaintops, but some animals travel almost to the peak.

The Snow Leopard

Snow leopards have a coat of thick fur on the pads of their paws so they don't get frostbite when they walk in the snow. They creep up silently and pounce on wild goats, their prey.

Snow leopards have extra-large paws that keep them from sinking into the snow, just like snowshoes.

The Yak

People who live in the Himalayas raise yaks. The yaks carry heavy loads and also provide milk to drink and meat to eat. Wild yaks, which live in herds, are now rare.

The yak's woolly coat keeps it warm, even in the freezing mountain temperatures.

Bearded vultures, which are endangered, live in the mountain ranges of Asia and Africa.

The Bearded Vulture

Bearded vultures fly through the mountains searching for animal bones to eat. When they find some, they carry them high in the air and drop them onto rocks to break them into bite-sized pieces.

The Andes

The Andes mountains stretch from the north end of South America to the south. A wide variety of animals live in the forests, plains, and deserts of the mountain range.

The Condor

The condor is one of the biggest birds that can fly. Condors glide high in the air, looking for dead animals to eat.

When condors are born, they are dark brown. Their feathers become blacker as they grow up. Only the adults have a white ruff around their neck.

The Spectacled Bear

Spectacled bears have light-coloured areas on their cheeks and forehead, and around their eyes. The pattern is different from one bear to the next. Spectacled bears often climb trees to eat fruit or to sleep.

Few spectacled bears are left in the wild because people have hunted so many of them.

The puma watches over its territory from high in a tree.

The Puma

Pumas are also called cougars or mountain lions. The hunters make great leaps from rock to rock when they come out in the morning and evening. During the day, they sleep in the shelter of a cave or hidden in the forest.

The Vicuña

The acrobatic vicuña (say: vi-KOON-yah) climbs steep rocks to look for a meal of plants. When threatened, vicuñas spit on their attacker!

Vicuñas are from the same family as llamas and camels.

The Alps

Many kinds of animals scramble over the rocky cliffs of Europe's snow-capped Alps. Others scurry about the mountains' meadows or fly over quiet alpine lakes.

The Ibex

The ibex is a wild goat that can cling to rocky cliffs with its hooves. Male ibex have long horns. When two males meet, they butt heads, each one trying to push the other. The first one to step back loses the contest!

Every year, the ibex's horns grow one ring longer.

The Eurasian Lynx

Lynx are very shy. They live in the forest or on rugged land with lots of hiding places. They come out at night to hunt snowshoe hares, birds, and small rodents.

Lynx scratch their claws on rocky surfaces to keep them sharp.

The Golden Eagle

Golden eagles fly in big circles, watching for young marmots or chamois. They dive down to catch the animals and carry them away in their long claws, called talons.

Golden eagles have excellent eyesight. They can spot their prey from high in the sky.

With the first snowfall, marmots huddle in their burrows and sleep all winter long.

The Chamois

The chamois (say: SHAM-ee) can jump high in the air and climb up bare rock walls. It leaps from one rocky cliff to another and never falls.

The Marmot

Marmots soak up the sun near the entrance to their burrows. When a marmot spots a golden eagle flying in the sky, it whistles loudly to warn other marmots, then scurries into hiding.

During the winter, chamois come down from the mountaintop into the valley, where there is more food.

The Grizzly Bear

Huge grizzly bears live in the northwest part of North America, far away from people. The bears travel long distances every year in their search for food.

A Hearty Appetite

Bears eat everything. Depending on the season, they eat blueberries, saskatoon berries, leafy plants, and roots. Salmon, frogs, and insects are also on the menu. But their favourite treat is honey, even if it means getting stung by a few bees!

Grizzly bears are giants. When they stand on two legs, they are much taller than a person – and very strong.

Bears have a good memory. They can remember the best places to find berries.

In the winter, the female bear gives birth to as many as three tiny cubs. When summer comes, the cubs discover the world by playing. Climbing trees is great fun!

In the Ocean

Fish share their ocean home with many different animals. This watery world is bursting with life, in warm water or in icy-cold.

At Low Tide

When the tide goes out from the shore, some water stays on the beach in pools among the rocks. A world of animals lives in these pools.

The Sea Urchin

Sea urchins hang onto rocks with their spines and tube-like feet to keep from being swept away by the waves. Some of the spines can move like legs, and sea urchins use them to creep along the sea floor or the sandy beach.

The name urchin comes from an old English word for hedgehog, the spiked animal that these prickly creatures look like.

Sea Stars

Hungry sea stars spend their days looking for oysters and mussels. When they find one, they crack open the shell with their arms. Sometimes they lose an arm opening the shell, but sea star arms can grow back!

Sea stars hide in the sand or cling to rocks.

The Common Prawn

Common prawns are easily frightened and will hide in a corner of the tide pool if a person tries to touch their antennae. These ten-legged creatures like to live in rocky shores.

The common prawn is see-through, with stripes all over its body.

The Mussel

Mussels have a soft body protected by a shell that is black on the outside and white on the inside. Mussels swallow and spit out seawater, eating the tiny animals they find there.

Mussels attach themselves to rocks using sticky threads they make themselves.

The Green Crab

Green crabs hide from birds that want to eat them by diving under seaweed or scuttling behind rocks. The green crab's sturdy shell gives it extra protection from enemies. Like all crabs, green crabs walk sideways.

Green crabs fight other crabs with their pincers (front claws).

Seabirds

Seabirds ride the wind, flying over the oceans
in any weather. Some seabirds never land on the ground,
except to lay their eggs and care for their babies.

The Gull

Gulls fly far out to sea. But when there is a storm, they come inland to fly over cities. Gulls like to gulp down fish but will also eat food that people leave behind.

When gulls build a nest, they stick it to cliff walls using their own poop as glue.

The Atlantic Puffin

Puffins fly over the sea all winter. In the spring, they lay one egg on a clifftop. To build a nest, puffins dig a burrow in the grass or move into an empty rabbit burrow.

Puffins ride on the ocean like ducks and can "fly" underwater, using their wings to swim as they catch small fish.

The Albatross

With their huge wings, albatross have trouble taking off and landing, so the birds spend most of their time in the air. They catch fish and feed on fish parts thrown out by fishing boats.

Albatross fly like gliders, using the sea winds to take them where they want to go.

The Northern Gannet

Northern gannets spend their days flying over the sea, sometimes in large V-shaped flocks. When a gannet spots a fish, it folds up its wings and dives headfirst into the water to catch it.

The graceful northern gannet is easy to spot with its yellow head and long, grey-blue beak.

Giants of the Deep

Enormous animals glide like birds through the deep ocean water.

The Humpback Whale

Humpback whales are as long as two buses and weigh as much as six elephants. To attract females, the male sings songs that can be heard underwater from far away.

Baby humpback whales stay with their mother for a whole year, always swimming by her side.

The Great White Shark

The great white shark is enormous and has super-sharp teeth. It can smell blood from far away. When the shark zeroes in on its prey of dolphins, whales, or fish, it attacks from below to surprise them.

Thanks to its long, sleek body, the great white shark can speed through the water.

The Green Sea Turtle

The large green sea turtle lives in warm seas. Green sea turtles always go back to the beach where they were born to lay about one hundred eggs. The round eggs look like ping-pong balls.

Green sea turtles are green because they eat lots of green algae.

The Dolphin

In all of the oceans around the world, playful dolphins zip through the water and leap over the waves.

Dolphins live in groups called pods. They hunt for fish together and protect each other from enemies.

The Dolphin's Smile

People say dolphins look like they're smiling because of their long nose and mouth full of pointy little teeth. Dolphins use their teeth to hang onto slippery fish and to defend themselves, biting attackers wherever they can.

Dolphins are clever and curious. Sometimes they come right up to take a look at people!

In the water, dolphins are speedy swimmers.
The playful creatures can also do flips
and somersaults.

Colourful Fish

In warm seas, coral reefs are like huge undersea forests.
These reefs are full of hiding spots for thousands of pretty fish.

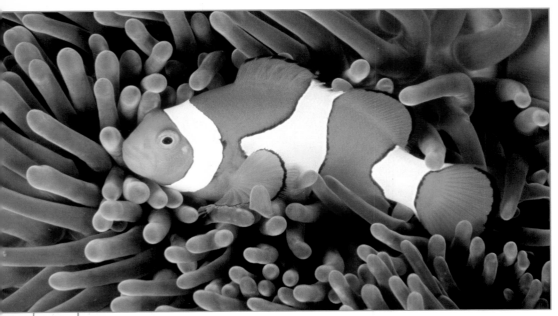

Clown fish build their nests in anemones.

The Clown Fish

Only the little clown fish dares to go near sea anemones (say: a-NEM-uh-nee), which can sting with their tentacles. Clown fish aren't harmed by the anemone's venom. The fish live in pairs among sea anemones, eating whatever leftovers they can find.

The Parrot Fish

This big parrot fish has a sturdy beak-like jaw that it uses to bite off hard pieces of coral. Underwater, the munching fish sounds like someone eating a crunchy cookie.

The male parrot fish can be red, blue, or yellow. The female is grey all over.

Clown triggerfish are not fast swimmers. But they can often escape predators that are trying to swallow them. They have big, white spots on their belly and yellow streaks on their head and eyes. These markings make them hard to see in the colourful reef.

The clown triggerfish uses its sharp spine to wedge itself into the reef out of its predators' reach.

The Raccoon Butterfly Fish

Raccoon butterfly fish have a black mask across their eyes just like a raccoon. They also have a big black spot on their tails that looks a bit like an eye. Enemies are confused and don't know which end is which.

Butterfly fish have comb-like teeth that help them feed on small worms and algae.

Strange Creatures of the Deep

The deep ocean waters are home to many strange, and sometimes dangerous, creatures, big and small.

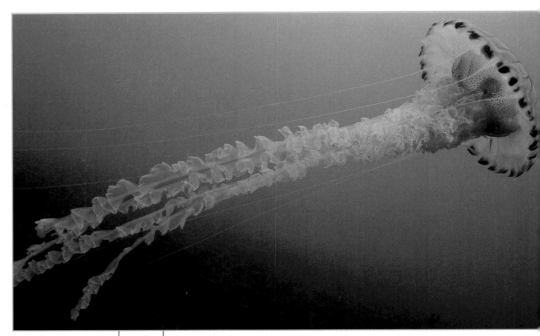

The Jelly

The jelly's body is soft and squishy with long, sticky tentacles that trail behind it. These tentacles trap fish with their venomous little hooks.

If you go to the beach, never touch a jelly. Even a dead jelly lying on the sand can sting.

The Seahorse

The seahorse is a little fish whose body is covered with hard plates. To keep from being carried away by the waves, seahorses curl their tails around a bit of seaweed and hang on tight!

Seahorses suck and swallow tiny creatures through their straw-shaped mouths.

The octopus has eight tentacles lined with suction cups.

The Octopus

Octopuses change colour to blend in with the sand or rocks. When threatened or disturbed, they spit out a cloud of black ink and swim away at top speed.

The Lionfish

Lionfish have long fins tipped with spines that they use to sting their prey. During the day, they lurk among the rocks. They come out at night to eat fish and shrimp.

There are many kinds of lionfish. This one lives in warm seas around coral reefs.

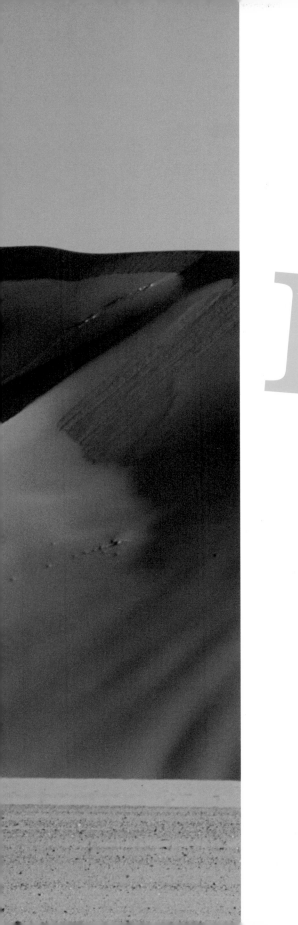

In the Desert

Only the toughest animals can survive life in the desert. Deserts are places with very little water and can be blazing hot during the day.

The Sahara Desert

Rain almost never falls in Africa's Sahara desert, the world's largest hot desert. Some animals in the Sahara live their whole lives without ever drinking a drop of water!

A scorpion's stinger is needle-sharp and its venom can be poisonous to people.

The Scorpion

During the day, scorpions hide under rocks. They come out at night and wait for crickets, spiders, or lizards to wander within reach. Scorpions never drink water. The moisture in the animals they eat is all the water they need.

The Horned Viper

When the sun gets too hot, the horned viper digs its way down to cooler sand beneath the surface. Only its eyes and two little horns peek out through the sand. It springs out of its hiding place to catch a meal of rodents and birds.

The horned viper hides easily in the desert. It's almost the same colour as the sand.

The Fennec Fox

Fennec foxes keep cool in the fiery desert by giving off heat through their big ears. Thick fur covers the bottoms of their feet to protect them from the hot sand. People train fennec foxes to hunt snakes and scorpions. The foxes sneak up quietly and pounce.

The small fennec fox is about the size of a cat.

The Camel

Without camels, people would never be able to live in the desert. There are two types of camel: bactrian and dromedary. They're different from each other in several ways.

The Camel's Hump

Dromedary (say: DRAH-muh-dair-ee) camels live in the hot African deserts. Bactrian (say: BAC-tree-an) camels live in cooler deserts and in the mountains of Asia. Both are tough, strong animals. Their bodies turn the water they drink and the food they eat into fat, which they store in their humps. The fat keeps them going when food and water are hard to find.

Dromedary camels have one hump. They can go for ten days without water. Then they drink one hundred litres (twenty-two gallons) all at once. That's half a bathtubful of water!

Bactrian camels have two humps. Their feet are smaller than dromedary camels' feet, and their coat grows long in the winter.

A dromedary camel can carry a
person or a heavy load on its hump.
It can walk for a long time without
suffering from the heat.

The Rocky Desert

Hardy animals make their homes in the rocky deserts of the southwestern United States. The dry landscapes have lots of tall cactus plants and big, red rocks.

When it can't find any tender grass, the jackrabbit eats cactus plants.

The Jackrabbit

Jackrabbits don't dig burrows, but they stay in the shade during the hottest hours of the day. When in danger, they hop away quickly in long, zigzagging jumps.

The Coyote

Coyotes look a bit like wolves, but they are smaller and live alone or in pairs instead of in packs. The noisy animals howl to tell other coyotes where they are.

Coyotes live all over North America, in deserts, forests, grasslands, and even in some cities.

The Great Horned Owl

When the great horned owl spreads its wings wide, it's almost as big as a ten-year-old kid. Great horned owls sometimes fly close to small towns where they might catch a duck for their supper.

Great horned owls take over the nests of other birds or will nest in a cactus plant.

After a cold night in the desert, the greater roadrunner fluffs up its feathers to let the sun warm its black skin.

The Greater Roadrunner

Although it's a bird, the speedy roadrunner rarely flies. It would rather run to catch its prey of mice, lizards, and snakes. Roadrunners kill their prey with a sharp blow to the head before swallowing them.

Deep in Australia

The Outback is a huge area in the middle of Australia. It's one of the driest places in the world. Most of the creatures living there aren't found anywhere else in the world.

The Thorny Devil

Thorny devils eat nothing but ants. The prickly creatures also have grooves in their skin that collect water and carry it to their mouth to give them a drink. When in danger, thorny devils keep perfectly still so their enemies can't see them.

Thorny devils turn dark greenish-grey when they're cold or frightened.

The Dingo

The dingo is a type of wild dog. Dingoes eat all sorts of things — bugs, rabbits, and plants. Sometimes they even attack kangaroos or sneak onto a farm to steal sheep.

Dingoes don't bark. They howl like wolves.

A curious baby kangaroo pokes its head out of its mom's pouch to look at the world around it.

The Kangaroo

With their powerful legs, kangaroos can jump far and high. The female gives birth to a tiny baby that stays safe and warm in her pouch while it grows.

The World's Coldest Places

Animals need thick fur and extra fat for life
in Earth's frosty Arctic and Antarctic regions.
These lands of ice and snow are dry like
the desert but very, very cold!

On the Tundra

The frozen tundra is a place where no trees can grow.
Summer is short and winter is icy cold. Animals living on the tundra
are covered with thick fur or warm down and feathers.

The Arctic Fox

The arctic fox is much smaller than the red fox and has smaller, rounded ears. Sometimes, hungry arctic foxes follow polar bears to snatch up their leftovers.

Arctic foxes have white fur in the winter and brown fur in the summer.

The Moose

Moose live in forests, as well as on the tundra. They have a broad snout and a fur-covered flap of skin, called a bell, dangling from their chin. In the summer, moose go swimming to graze on plants that grow underwater. The huge animals are less active in the winter, when food is hard to find.

Moose have the biggest antlers of any animal. They look like giant hands.

The Snowy Owl

Big, white snowy owls like to make a meal of lemmings. Lemmings are small rodents that live in the north. Male snowy owls are smaller than the females and have fewer black spots.

A snowy owl can turn its head backward to see what's behind it!

Some caribou are brown, while others are almost white. Both male and female caribou have antlers.

The Caribou

Caribou run in huge herds looking for grass or lichens to eat. Their large hooves help them run smoothly through snow and across the rough tundra. People often have trouble just walking on the same ground.

The Arctic

Earth's Far North is called the Arctic. It's so cold that a thick layer of ice, called pack ice, covers most of the sea. The animals that swim in the Arctic's icy waters are well padded with fat to protect them from the cold.

The Seal

Seals can stay underwater for a long time without breathing. The expert swimmers can change directions at top speed when a polar bear or killer whale is hunting them.

Seals have a thick layer of blubber under their skin to keep them warm.

The Walrus

Walruses have big, long teeth called tusks that they use to pull themselves along the ice. The males have longer tusks than the females, which they also use for fighting.

Walruses are excellent swimmers and often snooze on floating ice chunks.

The Polar Bear

Polar bears are the biggest bears in the world. The huge animals wander the pack ice hunting for seals. When they find one, they dive into the water to catch it. With their big, broad paws, they can walk on the ice without falling through.

The polar bear's thick, waterproof coat protects it from icy temperatures.

penguin or Auk?

Penguins are big birds that live in the southern parts of the world. Sometimes people confuse penguins with auks, which are northern birds.

Sea or Sky?

Penguins are too heavy to fly. But they swim so gracefully that they seem to be flying underwater. Auks fly quickly over the surface of the North Atlantic Ocean where they live. They use their sleek bodies and stiff wings to dive into the water after their prey.

Male emperor penguins spend the winter standing still on the pack ice with nothing to eat. They can't go looking for food since they're taking care of an egg. The egg sits on the penguins' feet, tucked under their bellies to keep it warm.

These razorbill birds are a type of auk. Most auks make their homes on cliffs, where they lay one or two eggs at a time and raise their young.

This fluffy baby penguin is covered with warm grey down.

Antarctica

The most southern place on Earth is called Antarctica. It's the world's coldest land, and animals make their homes only in the sea and on Antarctica's coast.

Male elephant seals, like the one pictured here, are five times bigger than the females.

The Elephant Seal

The elephant seal is the world's biggest seal. The huge animal spends its days in the water, hunting for fish and squid. Male elephant seals can stretch out their long nose to make their calls louder.

The Fur Seal

Fur seals have small ears and long flippers that help them walk on land. When a storm is blowing, fur seals look for shelter on the coast.

Fur seals hunt fish, squid, and krill, a shrimp-like creature.

Orcas have a white spot on the side of their head that looks like a big eye.

The Orca

Orcas make their homes in both cold and warm oceans all over the world. They are also called *killer whales* because they are fearsome hunters that sometimes attack dolphins and seals. They'll even tip over an ice chunk to catch the seal lying on it.

Index